CW00403081

GHOSTS

Anna Wigley

Gomer

Published in 2016 by Gomer Press, Llandysul,
Ceredigion SA44 4JL

ISBN 978 1 78562 132 1

A CIP record for this title is available from the British Library.

This book is published with the financial support of the
Welsh Books Council.

Printed and bound in Wales at
Gomer Press, Llandysul, Ceredigion

Acknowledgements

Thanks are due to the following magazines where some of these poems first appeared: *Amaryllis, Ariadne's Thread, Artemis, New Welsh Review, Orbis, Salopeot, The Interpreter's House.*

Thanks are due also to the Society of Authors for a grant that helped towards the writing of this book.

Contents

Contents (continued)

Chauvet

Deep in this palace of ice chandeliers
the bison huddle on their plain of stone.
A width of thirty-two thousand years
is no gap at all. There,
where a strong-necked horse ripples
through a haunch of rock,
footprints of a cave-bear wait
untouched by curiosity or storms.
And handprints clot in swarms
as witnesses: *I lived, I saw, I drew.*

Girl with Beret

on a portrait by Lucian Freud

I would love to touch your forehead
where the temples swell.
Or that shallow furrow
joining nose to lip.
There's a curl in that mouth
as if you're passing through
for money or the hell of it
on your way to some smuggler's den
or small-time pirate ship.
You're an urchin whose face
is clean as a snowdrop;
an artful dodger almost fledged.
The master caught you in his net
of lapidary light
where you still gaze out,
shunning all female feints,
binding your budded breasts.

Swedish Woods

i.m. Tomas Tranströmer

I have never walked
through a Swedish wood
except in these pages
where a blue darkness bushes out
in trees tall as cathedrals
and touches me at every point –
ears, heart, fingertips –
the resin leaving a sticky paw-print,
a glossy green scent.
And I never saw that wood
except in the circling raptors
of these lines with their hollow bones.
Here is the glove of snow
sheathing a branch, a slow
creaking in the white-breathed silence.
Here are poems like the intricate tracks
of hillock-hopping birds,
each toe splayed to show
that here there passed a creature
through the blank page of the snow.

Shrew

We find you –
a flung-away, cashmere thing –
among the scabious, heather and chough-cries
of Pembrokeshire's godly spaces.

Smaller than a mouse, softer
than a leveret,
you are lifted from your natural burial –
to rot into root and loam –

and folded in my coat like a fairy purse,
your thin feet perfect,
the thistledown of your pelt rich
as a Holbein ambassador's robe.

There you rest
in the shroud of my pocket-lining,
whiskers tickling at my hip.
When later I examine you in my palm

my mind cannot compute the smallness
of your transparent feet,
narrower than the blades of grass
they so lately, lightly, wove between.

Vision

Like a figure of snow, the cat
in the autumn street at dusk
loped with loose white flanks,
not hurrying for safety's sake,
while homecomers bustled and did not glance
at his soft, slow, radiant progress
towards the leaf-lined kerb,

small snow leopard in suburban stone,
one of God's rainy-day creations,
a fantasy in fur and silky light,
half liquid in his weightless grace,
his way of slipping nooses of all kinds;

and then he seemed to blend and fade
back into some shadow where my gaze
could not follow, his angel coat of dazzle
slipping noiseless among the gutters.

The False Black Widow

A monogram stitched in satin black,
you rested, a hand-span above the sink,
your bulbed body pregnant with threat.
We circled you, pupils as dark
and round as your fat black hump.
With those half-inch legs and pin-head eyes
you filled the room. The clock
ticked round your gleaming bodice.
By the time we got you shackled
between paper and glass, the evening
had drawn in, and there were owls
in the trees, and other things gathering.

The Owl

Seven times, the owl called outside your window
in the night; seven times you listened
as if the feathered ghost had called your name,
a summons from your world to his.
His first cry pierced the veil of sleep, and you heard it
as part of a dream; the second
made a dream of waking when you woke.
But his voice, claiming the dark fields,
making the moon-lighted lanes his own,
catching in its net your fluttering thoughts,
was for those moments more real than anything,
and made the room in which you slept
a strange and makeshift place, the furniture
a fiction fighting for its existence.
Then the cries stopped abruptly
as they had begun, and it was as if
the owl had never spoken, and never would again.

Number 99

young mountain lions in Alaska were tagged and
observed by zoologists to monitor their survival

Her ears were chewed off by the frosts
of her first Alaskan winter.
But how could she fail to thrive
with those padded fur gloves,
those Arctic-blue eyes?
Bulbed hook of her tail
navigated paths to safety, twitched
to sense shadows in the shadows.
Her infant growl was comical –
until we saw her snouting the tripes
of a still-pink carcass. She gripped
and tugged at innards still sweet,
then ate nothing for a week.
They found her after the second snow,
already hardened to an outsize toy,
her coat a tapestry framed in ice,
her muzzle closed for good
on the slender sinews of life.

Seamarks

to J.F.

You showed me the border places
where cliffs like healed scars
raised their welts
and earth gave way to rock,
a shine of wet shingle.

I think of them when I think of you –
the many creaking floors of sand
and the sun unfenced
in a wilderness of sky –

there were salt breezes
sweeping the gritty ballroom of the shore,
gulls blown off-course
and crabs the size of my fingernail
fumbling in rock pools.

It was you showed me the samphire
and the sea asters,
named the bleached thistles
and the long-toed birds.

I was not lost but found
in a landscape of washed skulls
and bruised stones,

the scruffy cliffs leaning
over my shadow,
the rolled glass of breakers
rushing forward to stain my shoe.

Pembrokeshire Triptych

Pentre Ifan

Led by trembling thickets to the spot,
we find the stones a hieroglyph in rock;
how to translate this windy house,
this tomb on stilts? It was not built
as riddle or curse, or road to the past.
The centuries glance off its sides,
the million sunrises framed
in its quadrangle sing
like the birds of Rhiannon.

★

Saint David's

Into this scooped shell of earth it fits
tight, like cockle or scallop.
Soft arches sing their praises;
amber-paved rooms
gleam with the passage of so many feet.
And echoes rise, diaphanous birds
that roost for a moment in the plaited timbers
then disperse, not graspable by us.

★

Seal at Porthgain

Climbing the dusty rope of track
that lassoes the cliff, we rise
above the shadowed throat of rock
where the hard waves smack and crash
to collars of white. The coast
snags our breath, makes everything sway
except the wiry gorse grazing our feet
and a lone gull's broad-tipped float
above the chasm. Then there,
where the churning slap of water stills
a little, a fat black whiskered face
parts the waves and shows itself.
Balanced on his muscled tail, he laps air
as a horse takes water at a stream;
four times he is swallowed back down,
then the sea is silk; he is gone.

A Cornish Wood

Once when young I walked through a wood
at night. The hour wrapped a blindfold
round my eyes. And yet, I was not quite
without some sense of mighty height,
leafy churches swaying in the dark.
Now I would go back there
to sip at that thrilling fright;
the way my skin became a pelt,
my fingers tendrils questing for a hold,
a word; my eyes like gongs
sheeted in black but shining nonetheless,
burning through the inky stuff.
How I reached the light,
the path, I'll never know.
It blossomed at my feet like
a ladder of pale beech planks
and, grasping the guy ropes, I climbed
aboard the ship, not slipping quite.

Creeper

Climb, climb the tower of this bush;
send out your ensigns to every outpost
of twisted wood; inch upwards
with your glossy, eager tips
through the old year's sheltering hood.
When I wake I want to see
ropes like pythons round that tree;
gorgons struggling to escape,
summer thrusting through the break.

Dreambird

At last I had got close to you
for there in a corner of the room
you were perched and purring,

folded on yourself in a perfect
self-holding, a handful
of tapering lines
and feathery calibrations.

You did not startle
or lift a wing in terror,
your poise was like
the balancing of diamond water

at the lip of a spring –
trembling, humped and braiding
but never quite spilling –

and then there were your greys
too numerous to name,
that gathered, glowed and faded
all at once, like rainclouds
filtering the sun.

You had no message, dreambird,
no grave annunciation.

Which grove of lower Elysium
you hailed from, I never learned;
perhaps you are roosting now

in some celestial currant bush
or visiting another whose sleep
calls to you with troubled lips.

Climbing my Father

You were castle and keep; I scaled
the walls to your battlements
and looked out at the world.
You were the wood's tallest tree:
I hung from the branches of your arms,
swung between chest and chin,
small hands grappling to get in.
Your heart was in there, a clock
made of oak, as ancient
and unsleeping as a star.
You let me explore your surfaces
and sunburn: I saw desert
on the back of your neck
and stroked the polished bowl of your brow.
You accommodated all manner
of hairs and wrinkles, gave shelter
to tussocks and tufts in your ears,
your delicate nostrils. You were
my first country to explore,
all your borders were open.
Your marmoset, I clung to you
with four flexible limbs
and breathed in tweed and tobacco.
I groomed your thinning hair
and even now feel its oil,
see its pewter, under my fingers.

The Lost Photo

And there you are at the age of five –
looking like a Victorian in Vienna –
hair flopping over a scowl
at the camera's demand for stillness,
sailor suit loose on your shoulders.
The lost world of my ancestors
shimmers its last frail atoms,
the patriarch stiff in his corner,
your father's upright father,
and the women trailing odours
of smelling salts and lavender,
the yards of starched linen.
But you – you are the very centre
of the tribe: the smallest
but the only future,
spilling from the edges of the frame
in a yearning to escape
to Attlee and Bevan, to a world
made of glass and air.

Snap

You are young and I hardly recognise you
gazing at a starlet in an open magazine –
the army has made you its own,
shaved you so those ears I stroked are cold.
You sit at a work-desk; behind you a map
being daily redrawn. Just what
are you thinking as you stare
at those red lips finished with a sneer,
the goddess eyes and gilded hair?
If I get through this bloody war
by God, I'm marrying her.

Grenadine

Sipping a glassful of grenadine
I taste in its rose window
the churches and cafés of Europe,
my father's Gaulois turning to ash
in the tray, my mother
still young, lifting the white cup
to lips painted pink
as pomegranate pips.

Rats

You were chasing Rommel, and I was chasing you.
Hidden in a fold of history,
somewhere between Normandy and El Alamein,
you smelt of sweat-heavy serge and sand.
What was it like? What did you dream of?
The Hollywood faces were taped to the hubcaps,
you feasted on them like the mirages that swam
real as photographs, in the dissolving distance.
I can hardly believe it was you, there –
brown as a hazelnut, guarding the tin-opener
as if it was made of diamonds,
cracking your teeth on the dog biscuits.
Did you sleep at all? Was the desert sky
still a poem, there in that dusty fortress
with the unexploded ground, the tanks
like charnel houses? You were twenty-six,
and older than I'd ever be.
Did you joke about the headless torsos?
I press the pages to my face,
breathing you in. The letters from Egypt
quiver in my hands in mummified remains.
Peering at camera footage I think I see
your face among the ranks saluting Monty,
then scraping away flies like black rain.
In Cairo you were suddenly rich,
waltzing on polished floors in a dinner suit,
feasting on delicacies with silver forks,
wealthy with water.
Did you dare to imagine a future
in which I walked towards you,
tottery on chubby legs, safe and fed,
with nothing to trouble me except
a fear of the dark, and a mouse-pain
from the sweet tooth you bequeathed me?

Cleopatra in Cardiff

In the half-light of the bedroom lamp
I am watching my mother dress.
It is already late

as she draws on the tissue-thin folds
of amethyst cloth
and cinches them at the waist.

On her silky forearms
gold bangles slide and clink
and her sandals wink

and flash as she walks
between mirror and window,
looking like a Manet

just risen from the couch.
This evening her smoke-black curls
are framing her face,

her lipstick's a ruby slash,
and as she bends to the glass
to soot her lashes with a brush

I catch a whiff of scent –
some stowaway from her past.
But most of all I'm anxious

for her modesty: that dress,
a fall of misty purple light,
makes her look more naked

than if she'd left it off.
She gathers up silver lighter,
cigarettes. Later,

I'll remember her swift visit
to my bed at midnight, the kiss
of opium in the dark.

Pelts

Her cashmere sweaters
seemed to keep her curves
even when she peeled them off
crackling with static as the hairs
fine as those on a young girl's lip
were brushed to a momentary frenzy
by her satin-skinned back.

They smelt of Yardley lipstick
and Silk Cut. They slipped
from her hands, loose as leopards
with a slither into the basket.

I could taste on them her life,
all of it: the tender hand-wash,
the wooden pegs, the coffee sipped,
the mascara tablet.
Her unlined silky cheek.
A bouquet of breasts and hips.

Scar

My mother's right thumb had survived
a beheading; it was cinched
beneath the nail. It had a waist.

I can see it now as she was knitting,
carefully drawing the yarn through the needles
with that understated grace.

I must have asked her how she got it
and she must have told me, once.
The scar was white and tight

as a torque. It gleamed
dully with details of a former life,
knew secrets I did not.

Glimpse

When she undressed for the bath,
the scar on her spine still fresh,
I was taken aback by the creamy satin
of her belly and breasts,
the rich curves like ripe pears,
the narrow span of her shoulders,
the collar bone sloped and delicate,
the gleaming hillocks of her knees
as she sat soaping herself.
It was almost too much information.
I saw not mother but lover,
not frame but picture.

The Journal

Her diary lies open in my hands,
the oxide of protective lies all cleaned.
The hidden treasure of her fears,
hope bubbling in an underground spring.
I finger the pages as an archivist
might barely touch a manuscript,
a gold and turquoise Book of Hours.
Her feelings are like coals:
they glow with dangerous heat.
I dread to read my name, to know the truth.
This worry about debt:
that stitches through the pages like a curse.
Money was the bandage I mislaid
– or rather never owned. I made
no bed for her to lie on,
no window latched against the cold;
only my useless palm across her brow,
some leaves stolen from her own garden.
And then there is the page where she calls
with anguish to her own dead mother:
how I wish you were here now, Mum,
and I could hold you in my arms –
to comfort her for great and little hurts,
to summon her back at last with all her sorrows.

Planting the Tulips

Post–Christmas,
the shop sells only these:

five Cinderella bulbs
still in their fireside rags –

their ripped winter coats.
I take them to be buried

and reborn; already
the soft yellow horns

are searching blind,
so with my rusty trowel

I part the wet black soil.
It is raining on my neck,

my hands, on the rich
embroidery of garden weeds

as I sink, scoop, shovel.
Easter is snug in my palm –

a handful of yeasty bulbs
set deep in the earth's flank,

the rain glazing my cheek,
my blackened fingers thrusting down

promises, the bland seeds
of filigreed ball-gowns.

To my Dieting Husband

Take these pears
the one fruit

you allow yourself
take this knife

and open the creamy hearts
wet with juice

the black pips
secret, glossy

and with dripping fingers
pare away the skin

of tarnished verdigris
the proud perky stalk

and press the grainy flesh
between your teeth

it slips
on tongue and lips

like honeyed rain
it leaves a stain

of syrup on your hands
your chin

on your plate
the stringy heart

a coil of jade
two seeds of ebony

Settings

If a table is well laid
with a linen cloth stiff
yet supple
clothing the bones of wood

and cutlery buffed to a slim dazzle,
the spoons pointing west,
the forks with eager tines

and the plates placed just so —
porcelain medallions
anchoring each guest —

and six broad glasses
like sentries awaiting orders,
are ready for the glug and splash,

and there where the cloth is smooth
as a lily's throat
you place a basket, a loaf,
for savour an eggcup of salt;

and you add to all this a candle
or two, the benediction
of wick, match, flame,

perhaps the last rose of summer
glowing from a bottle's neck,

you have, whatever your name
for its chapel, sacrosanct precision,

a supper worthy of the word,
a plain board fit for a king.

Papilloma

It was your most intimate gift,
the closest we ever got.

You loved me enough to pick my locks,
to rifle through my cells,

lay bare my DNA gold.
So stealthily you stole

through the corridors of flesh,
parting membranes like veils,

planting your foot at last
on the spot you loved the most.

It was a kind of kiss
I guess, a long goodbye,

a slow-slow-motion farewell.
Inside me it blossomed

and swelled. One day
I picked it like a cankered rose

and hid the slime.
Even now, your parting gift

stays with me in the small hours,
a tiny, potent stain

that you with bliss passed on,
passed on, passed on.

Dr Sherlock

He's on my case.
Tracking a trail of blood,
a scent of something spoiled.

With his magnifying glass
he'll spot the criminal cells,
the smashed windows.

Already there are tokens
of previous break-ins:
wrecked corners,

disarranged furniture.
He's calling in everything he's got –
the finest forensics.

When I wake up he'll tell me
whose fingerprints he found
and whether they cracked
the innermost safe.

Patient

The corridors of hospitals are like rehearsals
for the afterlife: the resignation,
the reckoning of one's sins,
the anxious, tedious waiting
for a sighting of St Peter.
We crowd like peasants in Flemish paintings,
dreading the trial, the verdict.
Heads bowed, shoulders stooped,
supplicants to the universe.

Excision

for Mr Lim

Limping, stern-faced stranger:
you reminded me of a Bond villain,
one with a Mao shirt and a metal arm.

You found out my inner secrets:
the creeping, untrimmed foliage,
the cells embroidered with rot.

Like a legendary princess I slept
forty days and forty nights,
and while I slept you worked –

trimming with your fairy blades,
your Thumbelina scissors,
sealing the cuts with fire.

When I woke there were signs
on my belly where you'd been.
Four of them, points of the compass.

I lay in my gauze of rescue,
still as a hiding bird,
palms on my sewn-up skin.

The nurses turned me upside down
and shook me. I survived.
I did not see you again.

Night Watch

Who were you, mute helper,
most tender and watchful,
visiting me all night like a bee
grooming lavender –

hovering, barely touching,
departing then returning
over and over, to my belly's
distended flower –

keeping my engine stoked,
my circuits running,
my very self balanced
like a dancer on one leg –

when I woke to daylight
you were no longer there.
Perhaps you had been a spirit
released from a syringe of morphine

or my dead mother,
come back for just one night
to cup my chin gently
proud of the water.

Gift

The suede skirt you gave me
slumped in its husk of tissue
like a sleeping puma, soft
as the coat of a dormouse,
heavy as a cobra,

brought a touch of the forest
to my suburban birthday,
a nose-thumb of luxury
to the crumbling rooms
of my fifty-two years.

Bonnard's Dogs

Submissive with excitement,
they flatten back chestnut ears
in readiness for the scrap, the pat;
or wait panting on bathroom floors
in a geode of dazzling tiles
for the mauve lady soaking in her tub.
They are copper and bronze, or the colour of peat,
with molasses eyes. So much at home
they seem, in this world of dropped towels,
of crumpled napkins and torn loaves,
of lamps casting nets of gold
for the catch of silvery sprats, lapis-washed mussels.

Passage

i.m. John

At last you lay translucent on the bed –
a wax doll, unmuscled to the throat,
brave bones gleaming through the tallow skin
at knees and hips. We watched and stroked
the naked labouring of your head,
the soft and faded surfaces
of the almost dead – all silver-white,
pale mauve and sea-washed stone.
You made no sound except the work
of forcing breaths through ragged lungs,
away somewhere inside the train
that carried you surely down the tracks
to who knows where. We thought
by gripping your hands to keep you there,
as if by the miracle of touch
we might stop the wheels and watch you
step down from the standing carriage.

Goslings

Already we waddle in miniature
on stumpy legs, our wings not grown,
the roots of them taped to our backs

as we paddle to keep up with mother,
our necks almost stiff as hers.
The humans stop in their tracks

and shower us with *aahs*
and crumbs of bread; but ours
is not to fill some heart-

shaped hole or need of theirs.
Out of their nursery books
we climb, dressed in capes

and ribbons and ladies' hats;
but our wet beaks nip,
our long throats are made to hiss.

Lesson

Three days you crouched under the lilac bush,
your asylum of twisted branches –
half-longing, half-fearing to step out.
I too crouched at a distance,
my young hand half-extended,
learning by instinct the lesson
that no wild animal can be caught by fright,
by trickery or strength; but must,
like the song from a blackbird's throat
be allowed to happen, not at once,
but at just that moment when it's right,
and the notes bubble up from the depth
of some sudden joy, unbidden breath.
So it was with you, scrawny cat,
all bedraggled with mud and soot,
your flanks as thin as pancakes,
as you huddled from the rain in your lilac house.
Not a moment too soon would you come,
not for me or anyone. I caught your eye
and flattered myself I'd caught you too;
but not by a whisker's width would you budge
from your sanctuary of dirt, though you starved
to a bundle of bony rags,
could have eaten a mountain of mice.
And so waiting was now a thing I understood –
not for minutes but for three rain-dark days –
my hand outstretched so it ached;
until in slow motion you crept forward,
treading the tightrope of your desire,
and crossed the border to my waiting fingers,
to a new world of meat and fire.

Tanya

You're flying to India again –
all seven stones of you, lithe
as a young silvered salmon,

face lifted to the rising sun.
Your hair will be braided
into rows of corn,

your feet breathing in the dust
of scorched villages,
your hands stroking the heads

of all those orphans
that will cluster round you
like the Von Trapp children,

admiring your strange blue eyes,
the freckles on your arms.
You seem to fear nothing –

neither distance nor harm.
The plush garden of Wales
waits slumbering for your return.

Cusp

That was the photo taken Before:
before things went askew and awry
like an eye that's not quite true.
In it my knees are raw and bone-awkward
under my gymslip; my figure's a boy's.
I wear the pleats, the sash and latticed shoes
of the paramilitary scholar –
on the hall table my glengarry,
in the wardrobe, my boater.
How happy I was with my satchel
fat as a doctor's bag, my knickers
of thick brown flannel that hugged my ribs.
It was all the discipline I craved,
climbing in procession the stairs
with their warped and silky stone,
keeping to the left always. Then treading
the hushed top-floor corridors
where only the priest crouched, waiting
to receive blushes and whispers.
I am petting our dog in the picture:
the red setter reckless on hind legs,
her whole body a joyful quiver,
her coat of copper feathers.
What I would not give to return
to that year when she was alive
and licking me pink with prickled tongue,
her belly on the bare skin of my thighs
like an armful of unbroken promises.

Bryony's Visit

You arrived like the past I wished for:
all shy confidence,
all legs and hair.

You made of your room a teenager's lair:
all mirrors propped,
all flimsy clothes dropped.

You lived on coffee and air:
your lips the sacred
portals, guarded with care.

You were always late, appearing
at the very last moment
on the stair

with your hair sleek and straight;
looking like a race horse
ready at the gate.

Tom

Was it really you
in that woven-reed coffin

with the nameplate so bright
it outshone the January sun?

Surely there was some mistake.
Because last time I saw you, Tom,

you were smiling and talking,
not a button or a shoelace

was undone. So how
could you be in that coffin

all silent and still and hidden,
when the last time I saw you, Tom.

you were open and upright and warm?

Emily Bronte's Bread

I imagine Emily's sleeves rolled back,
her hands floured to the wrist.
I think she would have kneaded hard
with strong brown fingers,
slapped the dough round the board
until it nestled like a partridge,
smooth and yeasty and plump.
Emily would have loved the song
of the swish and sift and thump,
her hair falling forward as she worked,
knocked back with a snowy forearm.
From the window she would have looked
onto starved horizons, a tree
crippled by caning winds.
As she put her bread to rise, her eyes
would have met those of a hare in the field —
before she, and the hare, bolted.

Waiting

My fine piano
still has all its teeth
and is longing
even now, at fifty,
to be ravished
by some classical cad
or jazz-playing johnny.

Pirates

When you disclosed your envy and your anger
I had to let it sail past me
with its flag of skull and crossbones
all scorched and tattered;
I had to feel the backwash from its hull
and not shudder. There were vultures
circling for my bones, so I reached
for my wine and took a sip
and did not catch their eye.
My coracle woozed on the eddies
and did not regain its balance
until my glass was dry.

Collecting the Casket

He had grown very light, after all.
We must remember that.
He was not quite as light as this casket
with its brutal nameplate,
but he had grown very light.
So light we could almost see his heart
struggling through the transparent flesh.
So light, his bones lay visible on the sheets,
his brain a honeyless hive.

And he had grown very small.
Not quite as small as this casket
with its tastefully polished lid;
but small enough for the child's bed,
the cat's chair, the flimsy commode.
Small enough to make his clothes
hang on him like blankets,
small enough to curl in our palms,
to slip through our desperate arms.

For Frances Horovitz

There was, about your face,
a strict, Plantagenet grace.
Like one of your own poems
its lines were true and spare:
delicate as a sparrow,
long and light as a hare.

Alison Moyet's House

Reading of how
with a diva's exhilaration

she spun through the house like a vortex,
singling out for special violence

the gold discs that gleamed like giant medals –
watching them crack under her hands –

I imagined my own life purged and emptied
of every last dust-collecting cushion and cup

and my rooms rising from the barnacling weight
into their own fine-boned dimensions,

light filling the space the TV had left,

and the house like a gallery at last
opening its new wing, the one

with the flight of curving stone steps
empty except for a woman's voice

unfurling upwards
towards the extraordinary light.

A Sunday Afternoon

I was fifteen that day in June
when my father brought you home –

an uncle in all but name, six-seven,
with small wet eyes and a potato nose.

I thought all men were my fathers,
their tweed lapels and brogues

proof of the fact, like the woollen bosoms
of my dry, untouchable aunts.

He was out of the room for a moment
and we were alone. Just a moment –

what can happen in that cat's-whisker
of time between exit and entrance –

and I marvel now at my girlhood
still intact: its smile

as I greeted you under the lights,
your bulk grizzly-like

and making the ceiling shrink.
By the time my father came back

I was turned away,
wiping my soiled mouth. You went,

leaving a tremble in my hands
as I stumbled out of Eden.

The Hour of Fred

to Simon

All guinea pigs were called Fred
but yours more so – more Fred
than any I'd seen before –
humped on your chest like a frightened lover,
with glossy toffee fur,
his eyes two drops of liquid tar.
You sprawled beneath him in a teenage boy's
languid self-spreading,
the two of you filling the whole settee,
as you stroked your prize pig with nail-bitten fingers.
His purring was prodigious, it shook him
like a speeding juggernaut, he
was in perfect pig paradise,
Fred heaven, as he crouched there,
black eyes closing on his own bliss,
until your face suddenly changed,
the stroking stopped, and you prised Fred off
the wet patch spreading on your shirt
like love, like embarrassment,
and back he went to his cold straw nest
in the outside shed – banished
until the next hour of pleasure,
the heavy warmth hugging your heart.

Stray

Little wilderness, not mine to explore;
    mad spark spat from a fire;
silky wrestler,
    chocolate-box predator,
sitting in a ruff of radar,
    of crepitations we do not hear,

she ripples through doors left ajar,
    scales with one leap of the will
a whole wallful of air,

    allows herself an inch to crouch
on the shelf's slim branch
    and blink there in her froth
of cappuccino fur;

    shows the throat-throttling pincers
of her glossy, natty maw;
    the ten switchblades she hides
in her gloves of white hair.
    She waits and waits and waits

for a nano-twitch, a telltale shudder,
    a careless bid for shelter,
a dust-coloured wing's flutter,
    an earwig's inaudible clatter
across the jungle clearing of the bathroom floor.

Girl Next Door

Two things I remember:
her laugh, an underground spring
tumbling up from some Bacchic joy
then spilling down, unbraiding,
as if she had been let into some secret –
she and the madman, the mystic.
It flowed from her without stint
or cause, a ribboned thing
waving streamers in the face of clocks
and compasses; of her mother's voice.
It had no strategy, no agenda;
but it taught me ever after
the power in a peal of subversive joy,
that nothing outfaces the tyrant
so much as that unstopped flow of laughter.

And the other was the sight
of her mother putting up her morning hair:
how she would sit with a cat's poise
in the upright chair, while that starry fleece
was yanked so savagely back it braced her neck
and rocked her in her seat. Her mother –
a Plymouth Brethren crow with tacks for eyes,
cat-o'-nine-tails in her mouth
to lash all naughty children –
dragged at the cape of brilliant strands
and screwed them into a knot that stretched
back the skin of her nine-year-old face.
With each scrape of the taloned brush
I winced, but not a hint of dark weather
spoiled the sunny morning of her face,
tightened the spigot of her laughter,
or left its dirty paw-print on her grace.

Sweet Sixteen

My adolescence sprawled on the lawn:
it squinted at the camera from the shade
of a thrown-back arm; a Rothmans
burned in its flung-out left hand
under that Seventies sun and lazy drum
of wasps caught in wine glasses. One
rested in sophisticated abandon
in the grass near my waist –
a kiss of *Hirondelle* on my lips,
my pores all plugged with hormone gum,
my head with the zigzags
that skittered along its corridors,
dropping silver bolts. I was fat
as a fishwife – breasts spraggling
through a cheap shirt, thighs
chafing under gypsy tiers.
Miserable and secret as a thief,
unravelling from my golden girlhood,
new vices worn like stripes,
hair worming through every border,
sweat blotting my chaste cottons.
A snake pit sunk between my ears
fed on nicotine and Mars Bars.
How ruined I was, in my palace
of infinite light, with its deep moat of years.

Still Life

on the statue at the entrance to the Bishop's Palace gardens, Wells

You stand at the gate but make no greeting,
enfolded in your own stilled essence —
grave spirit, bronze made grace —

a scarf of sorrow has blown
against your cheek,
has wrapped its fainting wing about your breast.
You borrow my breath

for a second: I'm treading cat-like
in your sovereign shadow,
making no flurry should I wake
you from your dream of inwardness.

Behind you the monkshood
and pampas grasses sway,
the roses spill their two-hundred years
of perfume. These walls

are heir to all the elements;
into their roofless hall and on your metal brow
fall cloudbursts of lonely rain.

The 600th Fire

over 600 hill fires were started during
April 2015 in South and West Wales

These burnt-out streets
receive the smoke we made;
it clings to every Poundland

and penny arcade;
it scents the hair
like rank pomade.

We're getting short
of earth to scorch
now it's May;

this may be the last
bouquet of fire
we offer

until next year.
There's nothing can beat
that crackling power,

that stink of threat.
We dream at night
of setting light

to the whole of Wales,
the pretty prison
flaring like tinder,

nothing but our glee
left unscorched
as the smoke hills gather.

Beast

i.m. Josh

Everywhere now I find his ghost:
a shadow that melts, silent and sad
on just that threshold where he used to sit.
It vanishes as I approach but then
a shallow indentation on the bed
teases me with reminders he was there
only three days since. He follows me
like a shade from ancient myth
through bathroom doors, up stairs,
the silk-padding stealth so light
I turn a dozen times to catch his step —
and find no actual trace except
unsmoothable impressions in my mind,
a new belief in spirits that are both
comfort and torment — the last
lost shreds of life, that haunt
a love so particular it shuns
all substitutes, except these ghosts.

Following the Pattern

for Jen

Inside you the cells are tying
their intricate knots –
their plain and purl.

You do not lift a finger –
your role

is smuggler, the one
who hides the booty in a bag,

gliding through Customs.
Your belly

will reach its true potential
now, no sad flatpack

but a burnished bowl.
Your craftsmanship

is remarkable:
just like that

you stitch another toenail,
a richly-vesselled rope of gut.

You told me you could not knit –
but here you are

turning out eyelashes by the dozen,
sowing a row of seed-pearls
under the gums.

You do it while you're sleeping and eating.
Your artistry is the real thing;

it will outlive you,
make your name.

Nancy at 6am

You tread the morning like a tightrope –
balancing frost-breath and car-snarl
under the light grip of your toes.
You place one sense in front of another,
trepidatious and bold, and the chill
snake of December circles your neck,
forces you to calibrate your quest,
tilt forward by an inch your fine-bored nose.
No gaggle of gasping crows
cheers you on, or tries with a stone
to knock you off your narrow beam;
only I, watching where I am not seen,
applaud your two-step past the currant,
your spirit-level gaze that draws
you paw-print by paw-print
through the leaf-lined, speechless dawn.